Little Earl Plays Guitar

This book belongs to

To my family especially my parents who saw something special in me before I could see it in myself.

To every little dreamer who bangs on pots, strums broomsticks, or sings into a hairbrush this is for you.

Keep playing. Keep believing.

With love, Earl Diamond

The Kitchen Band

Amazing music, wow! Little Earl loved making music so much that he started drumming on kitchen pots and pans! Can you imagine how cool that sounded? Bang, clang, boom! But after a while, his parents asked him to find a quiet way to make music. They probably needed some peace in the kitchen!

Little Earl just couldn't stop making music! After watching him play those pots over and over, his parents decided to get him something special a real drum set! How awesome is that? little Earl was jumping up and down with excitement, ready to make all kinds of cool beats.

The Broomstick Guitar

But wait, there's more! A few months later, Little Earl found another way to make music. He grabbed a kitchen broom and pretended it was a guitar! He would strum it and play songs in his imagination. Now that's what I call creative!

The Real Guitar Arrives

Little Earl parents saw how much he loved pretending to play guitar, so they surprised him with a real acoustic guitar! What an amazing gift! Little Earl must have been so excited to finally have a real instrument to play.

When Things Got Tough

But here's the thing about learning new stuff sometimes it's really hard! Little Earl tried and tried, but he couldn't make any music come out of his guitar. He felt frustrated and upset. Have you ever felt like that when trying something new? It's totally normal!

The Guitar Goes Under the Bed

Little Earl got so frustrated that he threw his guitar under his bed. He thought, "This is too hard! I can't do it!" But you know what? Every musician goes through this. Even the best guitar players in the world had trouble at first!

The Amazing Breakthrough!

After many weeks of practice and probably pulling that guitar back out from under the bed, something incredible happened! Little Earl played his very first song "Mary Had a Little Lamb"! He was SO proud and excited. His parents and Little sister clapped and cheered for him. What a special moment!

Little Earl Becomes a Real Musician

From that day on, Little Earl practiced every single day. He learned new songs, got better and better, and even started writing his own music! Every time he played, he felt like he was sharing something special with everyone who listened. Little Earl discovered that playing guitar wasn't just about making pretty sounds it was about telling stories, sharing feelings, and connecting with other people through music.

Your Musical Adventure Awaits!

Just like Little Earl, you might face challenges when learning something new. But remember every expert was once a beginner! Keep practicing, stay curious, and never give up on your dreams. Music is an amazing gift that will bring you joy for your whole life!

Author Bio

Earl Diamond is a passionate storyteller, musician, and creative visionary with a deep love for inspiring the next generation.

Drawing from childhood memories and musical adventures, Earl brings Little Earl to life with heart, rhythm, and a touch of humor. When he's not writing or creating, he enjoys encouraging young minds to dream big and make joyful noise wherever they are.

Copyright© 2025

All rights reserved. The contents of this book may not be reproduced, duplicated or transmitted without direct written permission from author Earl Diamond.

ISBN: 979-8-9931088-0-3

Trace And Color

Trace And Color

THE END

www.ingramcontent.com/pod-product-compliance
Lightning Source LLC
Chambersburg PA
CBHW060808090426
42736CB00002B/195